do?

HELLO

PLEASE

hank you!

May I take a message?

welcome

Nice

EXCUSE ME

HELLO

You're

you do?

Thank you!

PLEASE

A Little Book of Manners

EMILIE BARNES

with **Anne Christian Buchanan**

Illustrations by *Michal Sparks*

HARVEST HOUSE PUBLISHERS
Eugene, Oregon 97402

A Little Book of Manners

Copyright © 1998 Emilie Barnes and Anne Christian Buchanan
Published by Harvest House Publishers
Eugene, Oregon 97402

Indigo Gate
1 Pegasus Drive
Colts Neck, NJ 07722
(732) 577-9333

Design and Production: Garborg Design Works, Minneapolis, Minnesota

Library of Congress Cataloging-in-Publication Data
Barnes, Emilie.
    A little book of manners / Emilie Barnes with Anne Christian Buchanan;
    illustrations by Michal Sparks.
          p.   cm.
Summary: An introduction to the basics of good manners, from meeting and greeting people to proper telephone and mealtime behavior.
    ISBN 1-56507-678-8
    1. Etiquette for children and teenagers. [1. Etiquette.] I. Buchanan, Anne Christian. II. Sparks, Michal, ill. III. Title.
BJ1857.C5B347   1998
395.1'22—dc 21

          97-36915
          CIP
          AC

Printed in China.

01 02 03 04 05 06 07 / IM / 10 9 8 7

CONTENTS

"Please, Thank You, and Aunt Evelyn"

WHY I'M GLAD I'M LEARNING MANNERS

"Hello, I'm Emilie Marie, and I'm really glad to meet you."

That's one of the things my Aunt Evelyn has been teaching me to say. She's been helping me practice my manners.

I just got back from visiting at Aunt Evelyn's house, and that's one of my favorite places to go. Aunt Evelyn lets me dig in her garden and pick bouquets for our table. She lets me wear her hats and even play with her makeup. We bake cookies together and brew peppermint tea for our tea parties. And practicing manners—Aunt Evelyn calls it "etiquette"—is another fun thing we do together.

Don't be surprised that I said that.

Manners really can be fun!

It's fun to have pretend conversations: "Hello." "Goodbye." "I'm happy to meet you." "Thank you very much."

It's fun to set a table just right—knife here, fork there, napkin there (all fluffed up in a napkin ring), and a pretty bowl of flowers in the middle.

It's a lot of fun to go out to lunch to practice what I've learned! (I always order a grilled-cheese sandwich, and I eat it very politely!)

But fun isn't the only reason I like practicing manners with Aunt Evelyn. I also like what it does for me inside.

When I meet someone new, I like knowing what to say. When I go to my friend Donna's house to eat, I like knowing where to put my napkin and how to use my fork and what to do if I make a mistake. I like to feel happy and confident instead of embarrassed and shy—and good manners help me feel that way. People are nicer to me when I use my manners, and I like that, too.

Best of all, learning manners helps me have a kinder heart.

Aunt Evelyn says that's the real purpose of good manners. They're not just rules to remember. They help us *show* kindness and love and respect to other people, and they help us *feel* kinder and more loving and more respectful. Aunt Evelyn says they make life a lot easier, and a lot nicer.

One day she said it like this: "Love has manners."

I like that. I want to be a loving, polite person—and I know that you do, too.

So let me show you some of the things my Aunt Evelyn is teaching me about the heart of good manners.

MILIE

"Happy to Meet You!"

MEETING AND GREETING MANNERS

I love to talk! Don't you?

But have you ever noticed that sometimes the beginning or ending of a conversation is harder than the middle?

Sometimes when I meet someone new I feel all tongue-tied. Sometimes I feel grumpy and don't want to say anything (especially to my brother in the morning!). Sometimes I'm so excited and happy I don't even know what to say.

Then sometimes, when it's time to go, I don't know how to *end* a conversation, either!

That's when manners come to the rescue.

If you've practiced a nice, polite way to meet and greet people, you can get to that fun middle of a conversation without worrying too much about the beginning and the end.

Starting Off

It's always nice to stand to say hello, *especially* if I'm meeting somebody older than me.

Then I smile, look at the person, shake hands, and say something like:

"Hello"

or

"How are you this morning?"

A friendly "Hi" is all right, too, especially if I'm meeting someone my age. I usually like to say the other person's name out loud. This lets them know I remember who they are and usually makes them feel good. If I've just met them, saying the name out loud helps me remember it!

When I meet Aunt Evelyn, I always give her a big hug instead of shaking hands. I try to hug my parents a lot, too, especially when we haven't seen each other for awhile. When I see my brother in the morning, sometimes all I can manage is "Good morning," but that's important, too. I do the same with my friends.

It's nice to remember to say "Good morning" and "How are you" even to people you see every day and even when you're busy. Taking the time to say a friendly hello is really a way of saying, "You're important. I care about you."

Introducing People

Conversations are always more fun if everyone knows everybody else. If someone is new, it's good to introduce them. And it's nice to say something to help the people know each other a little better.

I just say something like:

"Aunt Evelyn, this is my friend, Chad. We go to school together."

or

"Donna, this is Anne. She lives down the street from me, and we go to church together."

It's polite to introduce younger people to older ones and introduce boys to girls. That means that I say the older person's or the girl's name first:

"Mrs. Klein, this is my friend Christine."

or

"Eileen, this is Bradley Joe."

What if a lot of people in a group don't know the new person? I just say something to the whole group like,

"Everybody, this is Yoli Brogger. She just moved in next door to me."

Then, if the group is small, I go around the circle and tell the new person the name of everybody there. If it's a really big group, like my class in school, I might ask them to tell her their names themselves. Then I stick around to make sure people are talking to the new person and help her fit in.

Introducing Myself

If I meet someone new and no one introduces them to me, I'm learning just to go ahead and introduce myself. That's kind of hard sometimes. I keep waiting for the other person to say hello. But if both of us are waiting like that, we might never meet each other at all!

It's really a lot better just to smile and say, "Hi. I'm Emilie Marie. What's your name?"

THAT'S A HARD ONE!

My friend Amy's mother wants me to call her Sharon. My mom says that's all right, but it would be better to call her Ms. Sharon. And I always call adults by Miss or Mister and their last name unless they ask me to do otherwise. Even then it's courteous to use their title with their names. Aunt Evelyn says it's a sign of respect.

If I'm greeting someone I've met before a long time ago (like my kindergarten teacher), it's still important to say my name. It's just not fair to say, "Hi, remember me?"—she would be very embarrassed if she didn't. So I just give a little reminder:

"Hi, I'm Emilie Marie. I was in your kindergarten class five years ago. I'm glad to see you again."

Breaking the Ice

When I'm talking to people I don't know very well, sometimes it's hard to know what to talk about after the hellos are finished. Aunt Evelyn says the very best way to handle this is to remember that everybody likes to talk about themselves. So I just ask questions and listen to the answers in a friendly way.

I mean general, get-to-know-you questions, like:

"Do you have any hobbies?"
"Do you like animals?"
"Where did you go to school last year?"

Asking questions is a good way to get a conversation started. Aunt Evelyn calls it "breaking the ice," and it's a good way to start talking to almost anyone.

A Friendly Chat

After the ice is broken and we're right in the middle of talking, there are still some things I can do to keep the conversation fun and pleasant for everyone.

One important thing is to include everyone

It's a pleasure to meet you

in the conversation. Whispering to one person in front of somebody else is really impolite, even if it's a very important secret and not mean at all. The people you're not whispering to may feel left out, and they may wonder if you're talking about them.

Another important thing to do when I'm talking is to listen. A conversation is not just what you say, but what others say, and it's hard to be a good listener if I'm always interrupting or thinking about what I want to say next.

Sometimes I'll get so excited that an idea will just blurt out while someone else is still talking. The thing to do then is to say:

"Oh, excuse me. I didn't mean to interrupt."
"I'm sorry. Please go on."

And sometimes (especially with grownups), it seems like they will *never* stop talking so I can say something. If it's really an emergency, I might interrupt with a very polite:

"Excuse me, but the house is on fire."
Otherwise, it's best to hold my thought until they're through. (I usually *do* get my turn.)

Of course, that reminds me of something else it's important to do in a pleasant conversation—which is give everyone a chance to talk! I hope I remember that when I'm a grownup.

Acting interested in the conversation is another kind of good manners. This is easy when I'm talking with my friends but not always easy when I'm talking with older people or people I don't find interesting. Even if I'm bored, it's not polite to yawn or look all around while someone is talking. (I wouldn't like it if someone did that to me!) When someone asks me a question, it's much nicer to answer with something more than "Uh-huh" or "Uhn-uh."

When it is my turn to talk, there are certain kinds of things it is better *not* to say. Aunt Evelyn calls this being tactful, and it simply means I don't say everything I think, especially if what I'm thinking might hurt someone's feelings. I don't tell Grandma she's fat. I don't blurt out that Suzie walks funny. I don't tell about the embarrassing thing that happened to my Mom.

HOW TO HAVE A HAPPY HANDSHAKE!

Hold your hand out with your fingers together and your thumb up.

Don't make a face if the other person squeezes too hard.

Don't squeeze too hard.

Don't let your hand go limp. No one wants to shake hands with a jellyfish.

Don't high-five or do fancy handshakes unless you already know the other person likes to do that.

If you meet a boy, you're the one who should offer to shake hands first.

Dirty jokes, jokes about certain groups of people, and any kind of negative comments about other people are not a courteous kind of conversation. They don't help anyone, and they can really hurt some people.

Finally, the nicest kind of conversations use those "magic" words we learned about in kindergarten. Everyone feels better when conversations are filled with:

"Please."
"Thank you."
"Excuse me."
"I'm sorry."

In fact, those polite words are just as important to use when I'm talking to my mom, my brother, or even Suzanne at school (who is *not* my best friend) as they are when talking to someone I've just met. Aunt Evelyn says that life goes a lot better when we make the effort to speak kindly and politely to everyone, but especially to the people we meet every day.

Saying Goodbye

When it's time to say goodbye, there's not really any need to hang around. All I need to say is:

"'Bye."
"See you."
"Thanks. It was fun talking to you."

STAY SAFE!

It's important to be friendly and to learn to speak up, but it's also important to be safe. It's not really a good idea for me to go up to a grownup I don't know and start to talking to him or her.

If the conversation just won't stop and I really need to leave, I can interrupt politely:

"Excuse me, but my mom's here. I've got to go. Goodbye."

I also like to tell new people I'm glad I met them. Just a few simple words will do it, like:

"Goodbye, it was really nice to meet you."

or

"I hope I see you again."

And you know what? When I've been using my manners, I usually mean just that!

DON'T MAKE A BIG DEAL ABOUT IT

If I notice something embarrassing the other person does not know—maybe she has something caught in her teeth or a big stain on the back of her shirt—I don't mention it in public. I wait until we're alone and tell her in a quiet, friendly voice. Sometimes I might say, "Excuse me, could I talk to you over here," but I don't make a big deal about it. That could be even more embarrassing than the teeth or the stain.

2 "Emilie Marie Speaking"

TELEPHONE MANNERS

Telephone talk is really just like any other talk—except that you and the other person can't see each other. You can't use a friendly smile or an interested face to help you say what you want to say. All you have is your words and your voice to give a message that is clear and friendly.

Aunt Evelyn says that's the heart of telephone manners. What I say over the phone should put a smile in the other person's heart!

Ring-a-Ding-Ding

What do I do when the phone rings? First, I say hello (not "yeah" or "whaddya want"). It's nice to say who I am, too:

> *"Hello. This is Emilie Marie speaking."*

If it's for me—hooray! Then I just talk. If it's for someone else, I politely ask the person on the telephone to wait while I call the other person to the phone:

> *"Just a minute, please, I'll get him ....Bob, it's for you."*

How I do the calling is really important. It's rude to just stand there and yell. The person who called will get her ears blasted, and besides, nobody likes to be yelled at! It's better to cover the mouthpiece (the part I speak into) with my hand and ask Bob quietly to come to the phone. If he's in the other room, I should put the phone down and go find him.

Aunt Evelyn says it's helpful to ask who is calling. That way, the person the call is for can get ready for the conversation and greet the caller by name. But just blurting out, "Who is this?" is not a polite way to ask. It's better to say:

> *"May I tell him who's calling?"* or
> *"Who is calling, please?"*

If I know the person who is calling, even if she's not calling to talk to me, it's always nice to talk a little before I go to find the person they called:

> *"Good morning, Mrs. Brogger. How are you? I'm fine. I'll go get Mom now."*

What if the person the call is for isn't home? Then I offer to take a message.

I find a piece of paper, write down the message, and put it where the person will find it. (In our house, we keep a little notepad and a pencil by the phone.) But even if I took a message, I tell the person about the call when I see her . . . just in case she didn't see the paper.

Emilie Marie Calling

When I'm the one making the call, I try to give the other person plenty of time to get to the phone. Aunt Evelyn says I should let the phone ring at least five or six times before I give up.

When somebody answers the phone, the first thing I do is say who I am—remember, they can't see me, and it's not fair to make them guess!

> *"Hello, this is Emilie Marie Barnes."*

I always give my full name unless I'm absolutely positive the other person knows who I am. (There are three Samanthas in my class, so there might be other Emilie Maries!) Then I ask politely for the person I want to speak to:

"May I speak to Donna, please?"

If the person I am calling is not home, I usually leave a message—an easy, short one! Once I left a long, complicated message for my friend Janet and her brother got it all mixed up—what a mess! So now I usually just leave my phone number.

Leaving a message on an answering machine or a voice-mail system isn't really any different from leaving a message with someone's mom or dad or brother or sister—except the machine doesn't make as many mistakes! I just wait for the beep (like the message tells me), give my name and the name of the person I'm calling, and leave my number and message.

"Hello, this is Emilie Marie and I'm calling for Bob. Please call me back when you can. My number is 875-4000."

Aunt Evelyn says I should always leave some sort of message on an answering machine, even if I dialed the wrong number and got someone else's machine, but I should keep all my messages short. And when I'm through leaving my message, it's always nice to say "thank you" and "goodbye" so the person knows the message is through—and to leave him or her with a nice feeling.

Wrong Number Blues

When the phone rings, I always hope it's someone

WHAT IF I'M HOME ALONE?

All of my friends know it's not a good idea ever to tell a caller we're home by ourselves. But what do you say?

My mom always told me just to say, "I'm sorry. They can't come to the phone right now. I'll be glad to take a message." I don't need to fib and say something like, "Oh, my mom's in the shower." It's best just to be polite, grownup, and calm.

I like. But sometimes it's a total stranger calling for someone I never heard of—it's a wrong number. Anyone can make a mistake, including me. So I try to be friendly and helpful to wrong-number callers. I say something like:

"I'm sorry, you must have dialed the wrong number. What number were you calling?"

Then, when the caller says "I'm sorry," I say, "That's all right. Goodbye."

If the caller just hangs up on me, I think, "How rude!" But that helps me remember not just to hang up when I dial a wrong number. It's important always to say "I'm sorry" and "thank you." Sometimes I tell them the number I was calling—I can figure out if the number I have is wrong or if my fingers just slipped:

"Oh, I'm sorry. I was dialing 857-4000. Is that your number?"

One thing I shouldn't do if someone calls my number by mistake is to give him my name or phone number. That's like giving my name to a stranger, and it's just not a good idea.

messages

First Person First

Do you have call waiting on your phone? We do in our house. If I'm on the phone and someone else tries to call our number, I hear a little beep in my ear. If I want to, I can put the first person "on hold" while I answer the new call. My mom showed me how to do it. I just press quickly on the little button that hangs up the phone, and then I can answer the other call.

Call waiting is nice when a really important call comes in—like my dad calling to say he'll be late. But call waiting can be a problem if I make the first person wait a long time while I talk to the second one. That's a little like letting someone cut in line.

There's another kind of "call waiting" that happens sometimes when I'm at a friend's house. We can be playing together, having a good time, when someone calls her on the phone. And then she has a long talk with that other person while I just sit there! That makes me feel like I'm not very important to my friend.

Aunt Evelyn and I have decided on a manners rule that takes care of both of these waiting problems: "First person first." That means the first person I am talking to—on the phone or in person—gets most of my attention. If anyone else calls, I'll talk just long enough to write down her number so I can call her back later.

Of course, if the second call is an emergency or someone you really need to talk to, there's nothing wrong with saying to the first person:

"I'm sorry, but this is a really important call. Do you mind if I call you later to talk?"

Good manners really mean thinking about how other people feel—and doing what you can to make them feel important and respected.

Some Do's & Don'ts

Speaking clearly and distinctly is a very important part of telephone manners. So is using polite words like "please" and "thank you" and "excuse me." Listening carefully and not interrupting is most important of all.

Reading or watching TV—in other words, not really listening—while I am on the phone is very rude. So is interrupting a phone conversation to speak to someone who is with you in the room. How can the person on the phone know who you are talking to? If I don't understand something, I should always say, "I beg your pardon" or "I'm sorry. I didn't understand that."

Some girls I know like to play pranks and jokes on the phone—like answering the phone in a silly way or calling up someone they don't know and asking joke questions or just hanging up on people. Jokes like these aren't funny at all. They waste other people's time, and sometimes they are even hurtful.

SOMETHING TO THINK ABOUT

When my great-great-grandmother was a little girl, there was no such thing as telephone manners—because telephones hadn't been invented yet. When my grandmother was a little girl, no one had an answering machine, so there were no special answering machine manners. The rules for manners change because times change. But the heart of manners is always the same: showing kindness and respect for others.

A Smile in Your Voice

Did you know that smiling while you talk on the telephone makes your voice sound friendlier? I've put a big sign next to our kitchen phone that says "Smile!"

Sharing the Telephone

In our family, we have four people, three telephones, but only one telephone line—and sometimes, more than one of us want to use the phone at the same time. Sharing a phone with other people means we have to be considerate of each other's needs.

Being considerate about using the phone means not talking too long when someone else needs to make a call.

It means not making a big fuss about waiting for someone else to get off the phone—and saying thank you when they do.

It means taking down messages carefully and remembering to deliver them. It means asking your mom or dad before making calls that cost extra—such as long distance.

It especially means not listening in secretly on one phone while your sister is talking on the other one—even when the conversation is really interesting.

I Don't Know What to Say!

What do you do when you don't know what to say over the phone?

Talking to my friends or my parents or Aunt Evelyn is easy. But sometimes I get confused or shy when I talk to grownups and people I don't know very well. I don't know what to say, so I just sit there.

Aunt Evelyn says that happens to everyone sometimes, but it's really important to learn to talk pleasantly with people I don't know. The talk doesn't have to be long, but it has to be more than just some grumbles and grunts.

It helps to practice, so Aunt Evelyn and I have pretend conversations. It also helps to write down a list of things to talk about over the phone. I did that with Grandma. I wrote down some things to tell her and some things to ask her about, and I put my list by the phone.

And you know what? The more we talk on the phone, the better I know her, and the less tongue-tied I feel. Now we have a lot of good talks on the telephone—just like I have with my friends.

That's the best thing about the telephone, I think.

It's a really good way to keep up with old friends and make new friends, too.

And all that works a lot better when I remember to practice my telephone manners.

MESSAGES

FOR
FROM

DATE
TIME

"Let's Go Over to My House"

PLAYTIME AND VISITING MANNERS

I really have fun with my friends from school, church, and my neighborhood.

But I never really thought about being *polite* to these friends—until Aunt Evelyn mentioned it.

She said that manners help me get along a lot better anywhere I work and play—even with my friends.

Remember that Aunt Evelyn said "love has manners"? Well, friendship has manners, too. The very best way to show good manners with my friends is to be a friend.

A Real Friend

Being a friend means being loyal and honest. It means keeping secrets and promises, helping each other out, and thinking about each other's feelings. It means being a good listener. And of course, being a friend means having fun and doing things together.

But being a friend *doesn't* mean whispering or telling secrets in front of someone else. It doesn't mean ganging up on someone or leaving someone out or making fun of someone who is not in the group.

Saying bad things or lying about other people is always bad manners—even when I'm mad. I can really hurt other people by telling stories about them. Even telling true stories—to a parent, teacher, or someone else my age—can be impolite if I use those stories just to get my own way or make someone else look bad.

Being a polite person means treating everybody with everyday good manners, even unpopular people or people who act strange or weird. I don't have to be everyone's best friend. But I should try to treat everyone I meet with kindness and respect. That means not making fun of people or laughing at them.

When we're playing games, good manners means being a good sport—not cheating, not using mean language, not bragging when I win or pouting when I lose. Everybody wins sometimes and loses sometimes. What's important is for all of us to do our best, encourage each other, and have fun—whether we're playing soccer, Monopoly, or Tic-Tac-Toe.

Making a Friend Welcome at My House

One of my favorite things to do with my friends is go over to each other's houses. Sometimes we go over to play for the afternoon. Sometimes we get together to do homework or to work on a project. Sometimes we have sleepovers, which are really fun.

No matter how long the visit, having a friend over to my house requires a special set of good manners. Aunt Evelyn calls this kind of manners "hospitality." It means making my guest feel welcome and special and helping her have a good time at my house.

Hospitality manners start with meeting my guest at the door or even in front of the house and saying, "Hi, come on in."

I show her where she can put her coat and her things, and I show her where the kitchen and bathrooms are. I introduce her to my family if she doesn't already know them, and I tell her about any house rules she needs to know.

After that, it's always polite to offer my guest something to eat or drink. Even if I don't have any juice or raisins or my mom doesn't want me to have a snack right then, I should at least offer my friend a drink of water.

Showing hospitality to my guests also means putting them first while they're over at my house. I offer them the biggest cookie, the best chair, and (if they're staying overnight), the most comfortable bed. And I try to do what they want to do (most of the time).

I don't say:

"This is my house, so we're going to do what I want."

Instead, I say,
"You're the guest. What do you want to do?"

One special part of hospitality means sharing my things with visitors. If she wants to play with my toy horses or my dolls, I should let her. If there is something special I don't want her playing with, I should ask my mom to help me put it away before my guest arrives.

IS MY BROTHER (OR SISTER) MY FRIEND?

I see my brother every day. I play with him sometimes. And sometimes he really makes me mad. Do I really have to mind my manners with him, too? Hard as it is, the answer is yes! Being polite to my brother means not teasing, tattling, or bickering. It means not counting chores or worrying about who is the "favorite." It means not saying mean things that hurt his feelings. It also means sticking up for him and helping him out and even, sometimes, giving him a hug. And no, I don't always act that way to my brother. He doesn't always act that way to me. But it's important to try. Aunt Evelyn (who is my mother's sister) says that treating a brother or sister kindly and with respect may even be more important than treating a friend that way. After all, we will probably know each other for a lot longer. Besides, it doesn't make sense to treat strangers and friends with kindness and respect and not act that way to our very own family!

15

If my guest is staying overnight or even longer, there are a few more things I can do for her. If she forgot her pajamas, I lend her some of mine. (My mom also keeps extra toothbrushes and stuff in case visitors forget theirs.) I make sure she has a comfy pillow to sleep on and a doll or stuffed animal to snuggle, and I ask her if she needs a nightlight. I ask her what she likes for breakfast. And I do whatever I can to help her feel right at home. That's really what hospitality—and good host manners—means.

Being the Guest

If I'm visiting at someone's house, my *manners-job* is a little different. My job is to fit into my friend's household and make it easy for her *family* to have me as a guest. It's also important to show that I appreciate their hospitality.

One thing that is very nice to do when I visit someone's house is to bring a little gift for her family. This kind of gift is called a "hostess gift." This isn't necessary if I just go over to Barbara's house for the afternoon, but it's a nice thing to do if I'm invited to dinner or to spend the night. A hostess gift doesn't have to be fancy or expensive. It can be a candle or a little plant or some cookies you baked or some flowers you picked from your garden. My mom or Aunt Evelyn always help me choose a nice gift to bring when I go to visit.

Whether I bring a gift or not, I always owe my hosts the gift of my respect and thanks. It is nice of them to let me come over. I should tell them so, and I should also show my respect by the way I act.

Remembering to wipe my feet at the door is a part of showing respect for my hosts. So is hanging up my coat and keeping my other belongings out of the way. I show respect by keeping my feet off the furniture and my hands off ornaments and decorations. I don't turn on the TV, the radio, or the VCR unless I'm invited to. And I help clean up any mess we make while we are playing.

It's also important to respect the privacy of my host and her family. Even though she is sharing her house with me, that doesn't give me the right to open drawers, peek in closets, or read private papers, no matter how curious I am. I certainly shouldn't use their things or try on their clothes without being invited to!

What should I do if I need something? There's nothing wrong with asking for a tissue or a drink of water, but I shouldn't demand things like snacks or treats. Instead, I should wait for my hosts to offer something. If what they offer is not my favorite, I shouldn't say so or ask for something else. I should just say thank you and enjoy the company of my friend.

If I'm invited for a meal, all my best mealtime manners apply. I should try to have a nice conversation with my friend and her family. I should also offer to help with setting the table, preparing the meal, or cleaning up.

One thing I should never say as a guest is "At my house we…." That sounds like my hosts' house isn't good enough, and it makes them feel bad. Besides, I'm not at my house! I'm in their house, and that means I follow their house rules—for bedtime, chores, and anything else.

If I'm staying overnight or several days, it's even more important to try to fit in with the way the household works. I should pick up after myself and not leave my things lying around. I should fold my towels neatly and hang them up, not leave them wadded on the floor. I should help my friend clean up her room, too. I should always knock before opening a closed door.

The heart of visiting manners is to be a thoughtful host and a thankful guest.

And we should both try to keep the noise level down, even if we're giggling in our rooms late at night. Sometimes it is hard to get to sleep when I'm having a sleepover …but we shouldn't keep the other people in the house up all night.

When it's time to leave, I shouldn't wear out my welcome by hanging around. Most important of all, I need to say a big thank-you to my friend and her family.

"Thanks for having me. I'm glad I came!"

"And I'm really glad that you're my friend."

A Good Host

Makes a guest feel welcome.
Offers something to eat and drink.
Helps the guest know what to do.
Shares with her guest.
Puts the guests' needs first.

A Good Guest

Doesn't complain or demand.
Doesn't snoop.
Follows house rules.
Picks up after herself.
Always says thank you.

The Heart of Good Manners—Every Day

Some kinds of manners are for special situations and special occasions, but other kinds of manners are good for any time. They make life easier and nicer and a lot more comfortable—and they help make special occasions more special. In fact, these everyday "to do" rules are the heart of all other good manners.

DO use polite words. "Please," "thank you," and "excuse me" are like sprinkles of sugar that make all my words and actions a little sweeter.

DO show respect for grownups and people in authority. Parents, teachers, pastors, policemen, and other grownups should be obeyed and honored. Arguing, talking back, and being disrespectful (even behind their backs) is bad manners.

DO be honest. Lying and cheating are not only wrong; they're also impolite—the very opposite of kindness and respect.

Don't say everything you think. If you hate your friend's new dress or you think your mom's new haircut is ugly or you notice that your teacher has a wart on her nose, you *don't* have to say so. Often you can just not say anything at all.

PLEASE

DO notice people's needs and try to help. If I see a little child who has dropped a toy, I pick it up. If an older person doesn't have a place to sit, offer her your seat. If someone's arms are full of books and packages, hold the door open for them.

Do practice saying, "After you." Let other people go through doors first or have the first choice. Your turn will come.

Do keep personal things personal. There are some personal things we all do (like burp, for example) that others *don't* want to watch us do or hear us talk about them. If you have to do something personal, excuse yourself and go to the bathroom. If you or someone else makes a mistake, don't giggle or laugh. Just say a quiet "excuse me" or ignore what happened and don't mention it again.

Do show consideration for others. Being considerate means being respectful of other people's property, other people's time, and other people's rights. Cover your mouth when you sneeze and cough. Keep the noise down when others are trying to rest. Ask before using something that doesn't belong to you. Pick up after yourself.

Thank you

how are you?

Do apologize when you need to. If you realize you have said something hurtful or done something thoughtless, say "I'm sorry" or "Excuse me."

Do respect others' privacy. Some things just aren't any of your business. It's impolite to read someone else's mail or diary or to look around in someone's purse, drawers, or closets unless they invite you to.

Don't point out other people's bad manners! This is really important. You're supposed to mind your manners, not your friends' manners or even your big brother's manners! It's better just to say nothing—even when someone does something really disgusting.

4 "Please Pass the Sugar!"
MEALTIME MANNERS

Have you ever wondered why there are so many "table manners" rules?

I have. So I asked my Aunt Evelyn why it's so important to do things like keep our elbows off the table and chew with our mouths closed.

She said we need table manners because mealtime is so important. It's when we feed our bodies with food. It's also when we feed our spirits with love and friendship. And it's easiest to do that when meals are peaceful and happy.

That's what table manners are really for—keeping mealtime nice for everyone.

Setting the Table

Mealtime manners really start before mealtime, with setting the table. Sometimes that's my job. Other times, the table is set for me and my job is to know what to do with the plates and the knives and the forks.

Either way, table settings are easy (and fun) once you know the basics about what goes where.

First comes a tablecloth or a placemat. Next comes something pretty in the middle—maybe some flowers in a bowl or some little candles in pretty holders. And then we have the place settings—the plates and knives and forks. Here is a picture of a simple one, the kind I make when I'm setting the table for family dinners:

The dinner plate goes in the middle, with the eating utensils on either side. The knife and spoon are on the right, with the knife closer to the plate and facing in. The forks are on the left, with their prongs facing up. The napkin is usually on the left, too, or it may go on the plate or even in a glass. Glasses and cups go a little above the plate—toward the middle of the table—and on the right side. (An easy way to remember this is that the word drink begins with "DR"—"Drinks Right.")

Aunt Evelyn actually made me a place-setting placemat to help me remember where to put everything. You can make one, too. Just copy the picture onto a big piece of construction paper, and cover it with clear adhesive-backed plastic. You can actually use it as a placemat, or you can just use it to help you remember how to set the table.

Of course, sometimes place settings get a lot *fancier*. Sometimes there is a separate salad plate and a bread-and-butter plate. Sometimes there are water glasses and glasses for other beverages, or cups for tea or coffee. Sometimes there are three forks and two spoons. But the same basic rules still apply—dinner plate in the center, forks and napkins left, knives and spoons right, drinks right, plus extra plates go on the left.

Knowing these rules helps me when I go to a restaurant or somebody's house and I don't know how what to do with part of my place setting. The main rule to remember is that the things you use first go on the outside, farthest from the plate. That means the napkin is farthest left because you pick it up first, then little forks for fish or salad, and finally the dinner fork. On the right, the soup spoon is farthest right, then the teaspoon and the dinner knife.

If I'm not sure what to do, I just watch the people around me and do what they do.

> The heart of mealtime manners is to act so that everyone at the table (including you!) can enjoy the food and the company.

A Mealtime Blessing

Dear God, thank you for this good food. Thank you for our family and friends. Thank you for loving us. Amen.

Dinner Is Served

The first thing I do at dinnertime comes before I actually come to the table—I wash my hands! Then I go to the dinner table and wait for everybody else to come, so we can sit down together. At home I always know where my place is. If I'm visiting, I wait for my hostess or host to tell me where to sit—or I look for a place card. Then I wait for the hostess to sit down before I do.

In our family, we always say a blessing—a little thank-you prayer—before we eat. We hold hands and take turns saying it. My friend Yolanda's family calls it "saying grace," and her father usually does it. My friend Jessica's family doesn't say grace at all, but she always bows her head politely with us when she eats over at my house. (When I'm at her house, I like to say a quiet little thank-you prayer inside my head before we start.)

Then I pick up my napkin and place it in my lap. (I never flap it open or tuck it in my shirt like a bib.) If it's a big dinner napkin I leave it folded in half, with the fold toward me.

If the food is served family style, I pick up the dish nearest me and offer it to the person on my right. When a dish is passed to me, I serve my plate, return the serving spoon to the dish, and pass it to the person on my right. I try to pay attention to how much food there is and how many people are at the table—I don't want to take so much that somebody doesn't get enough. I don't pick through the dish to find the best piece; I just take what is nearest to me. And if I am asked to pass a glass or a cup, I only touch the outside, not the rim.

Sometimes food is served "buffet style," which means I go to a different table and serve myself from a lot of different dishes. The most important thing to remember about serving myself at a buffet is not to put too much on my plate. It's better to start with small amounts and go back to the buffet table if I want seconds. I also need to remember not to touch anything that is not actually going on my plate and not to take too much of one dish.

What If I Don't Like It?

Almost everybody has certain foods they don't like. I can't stand broccoli. My friend Donna doesn't like meat loaf. Jessica is allergic to milk and milk products.

So what do we do if we go over to Yoli's house for dinner and find ourselves looking at bowls of meatloaf, broccoli with cheese sauce, and mashed potatoes?

What we *shouldn't* do is look at the food on the table, make a face, and say, "Yuk" or "I can't eat that."

There are lots of better ways to handle the situation.

We can simply say "No, thank you" when the food is offered. Even better, we can say, "Just a little, please" or just take a very small serving from the bowl. Then we can eat just a few bites.

What if you're allergic to something and *can't* eat it? My friend Barbara, who is very allergic to peanuts, quietly lets the hostess know. And if she can, Barbara explains about her allergy before she goes over to eat.

Making Mealtimes Pleasant

Mealtimes are nicest when everyone starts and finishes at about the same time. So I wait for the hostess (or my mom) to start before I do, and I try to eat at about the same pace as everybody else.

How I sit at the table can make a difference in how pleasant a meal is for me and others. I try not to rock my chair or move around too much—that's distracting to others and might cause spills. And I try to sit up straight with my elbows at my side (not on the table) and my hands in my lap when I'm not using them. This looks nicer, helps food go down better, and

FAST FOOD MANNERS

Mealtime manners are for everywhere—even in a burger or a taco place. Fast food restaurants even call for some special kinds of manners. It's important to be courteous to the person who takes my order. It's also good to think ahead about what I want so I won't hold up the line while I try to decide what to order. I shouldn't take more napkins, straws, or condiments (ketchup, mustard, relish) than I need, and of course I should use good manners while I'm eating. (Chewing with my mouth open is just as disgusting in a Burger Palace as it is at home.) Finally, I should throw away my trash when I am through and leave my table clean for the next people who eat there.

even helps keep my clothes clean.

Pleasant conversation is also an important part of mealtime—as important as eating. But conversation and eating shouldn't happen at the very same second! If I chew first, swallow, and then talk, people won't have to look at a yukky mouthful of chewed food. (I try to chew with my mouth closed.) All this is easier if I remember to take small bites and sips instead of big gulps and forkfuls. And I should never wave a fork or a piece of carrot around in my hand while I talk.

Another way to keep mealtimes pleasant for everyone is to eat quietly (without chomps and slurps), and to remember to use polite language.

What to Do with a Knife & Fork

There's a polite way to eat almost any food. We eat most foods, of course, with a fork. In America, we hold forks and spoons like pencils, scooping our food onto the utinsils.

If I'm served soup, I tip the spoon away from me, scoop up a little soup, and sip it from the side of the spoon. It's all right to tilt the bowl away from me to get the last of the soup, but I shouldn't pick up the bowl and drink it. And I should never, *ever* slurp!

Bread goes on the bread-and-butter plate if there is one, or just on the side of the plate. When the butter is passed, I put a little bit on my plate and use it to butter pieces of bread as I eat them. I shouldn't butter my bread all at once. It's better to break off a small piece, butter it, then eat it.

The same thing goes for meat. Instead of cutting it all up

into little pieces first, I cut off each piece before I eat it.

Sometimes salad comes in big pieces that are messy to put in my mouth. Aunt Evelyn said it's OK to cut the lettuce into smaller pieces with a knife and fork.

It's all right to eat some foods with your fingers: grapes, plums, cherries, celery, carrot sticks, pickles, olives, radishes, corn on the cob, crab and lobster claws, artichokes, and dry, crisp bacon. (Be sure and clean your fingers with a napkin afterwards.)

French fries and fried chicken can be eaten with fingers at a picnic or a fast-food restaurant, but they should be eaten with a fork (or knife and fork) in a dining room.

And what about pizza, which is my all-time favorite food? Most of the time it's all right to eat it with my hands. In a nice restaurant, or if the pizza is really gooey and cheesy, I use a knife and fork.

Once I've picked up a knife, fork, or spoon, it should never go back on the table. When I'm not using it, it should rest on the edge of my plate—the whole thing, not just the eating part. Soup spoons should be left in the bowl or on the plate that comes under the bowl.

If Something Happens

Mealtimes don't always go smoothly. Sometimes I'll spill something or get something stuck in my mouth or even make an embarrassing sound. Aunt Evelyn says the best thing to do with situations like these is to take care of them quietly. If I knock over my glass, I just say "I'm sorry" and help clean up the mess. If I burp or my stomach growls, I just say a quiet "Excuse me" and go on with my meal.

What if something ends up in my mouth that I don't want—like a bone or a piece of gristle or something that's too hot or tastes really awful? It's never polite to just spit it out.

If it's too hot, I can take a drink of water. If it tastes bad, I should swallow it quickly and take a bite of something else. If it's something I *can't* swallow, I can remove it with my fingertips or the tip of my fork and place it on the side of my plate.

If I have something stuck between my teeth or some other problem I can't take care of pleasantly at the table, I ask to be excused and then take the problem to another room. (When I leave in the middle of a meal, I should leave my napkin on my chair.)

Finishing Up

I always feel good when I've finished a nice meal. My tummy is satisfied, and I've had a nice time talking to my family and friends. What do I do then?

First, I wait for everyone else to finish—or at home, I may ask politely to be excused. Then I place my knife, fork, and spoon side by side in the middle of my plate with the tines of the fork pointing down. I place my napkin loosely (not folded) beside my plate, and I push back my chair carefully.

It's nice to offer to help clean up. (At home, I always help.) But no matter what else I do, there's one important part of table manners I should never forget. That is saying "Thank you very much" to the one who made the meal.

DID YOU KNOW?

There's a reason we only butter a little piece of bread at a time. People used to eat from one big loaf, and what was left was given to the poor. If each person broke off only what they could eat at a time, none of the bread was wasted.

"I'm Really Glad You Came"

PARTYTIME MANNERS

"It's time for a party!"

Those are words I'm always happy to hear.

Sometimes I'm the party-giver. And sometimes I'm a partygoer. Either way, parties are fun—and they're a great place to practice good manners.

Partytime manners are not really hard to learn. Mostly they're just everyday good manners and mealtime manners and visiting manners all combined with an extra spark—making sure everyone has a special good time.

Making Party Plans

If I want to give a party of my own, the first thing I need to do is check with my parents and maybe some other adults. Not only is this polite, but I need their permission and their help! We need to talk together about what kind of party it will be, where it will be held, and how many people I can invite.

Once those important things have been decided, I can start planning. I really like this part of being a party-giver.

First, I need to think about party food and decorations and activities. I need to pick a theme and decide whether the party will be at home or somewhere else, like a park or a restaurant. Parties at pizza places, amusement parks, or gymnastics places are very popular. But I think that home parties can be even more fun—I actually get to spend more time with my friends.

Sometimes I like to have a very small tea party with just four or five guests. (I've even had tea parties for two.) Other times I invite a bigger group. I think it's fun to invite people I know from different places and help them get to know each other, too.

If my party is going to be small, I usually just invite a few of my good friends. If it's big, I try to invite all of one group of people—my whole Brownie troop or all the girls in my class. That way, people's feelings don't get hurt by being left out.

Please Come

If my party is going to be very casual, like a sleepover with a few friends, I usually just call them on the phone and invite them—or sometimes my mom calls their mother.

For a bigger or fancier party, though, it's better to send out written invitations. These can be plain or fancy, cute or serious, and I can make them by hand or fill in the "blanks" on ready-printed invitations. I usually like to make my own because it's fun. I fold a piece of construction paper, cut it in a fancy shape without cutting through the fold, decorate the outside, and then write the invitation on the inside.

The heart of partytime manners is to help everyone have a special good time.

On some occasions when I am older, Aunt Evelyn says—like graduations and weddings—I will want to send out formal engraved invitations. That means they are printed in a special way following certain special rules. For now, though, all I really need to worry about is making sure my invitations tell my friends what they need to know. An invitation should tell who is giving the party (me), what kind of party it will be, when the party will be held, and where it will be. It can also tell about special clothes guests should wear and things they should bring, and whether they need to tell me they are coming.

For example, when I gave a special garden tea party for five of my friends, I cut out little invitations in flower shapes and wrote this on the inside:

Please come to a special garden tea party
on Saturday, the fourteenth of June
at Emilie Marie Barnes's house
2838 Rumsey Drive
Please wear Sunday clothes and a pretty hat.
RSVP 682-4714

I added the "RSVP" and the phone number because I wanted my friends to call me and say whether they were coming or not. "RSVP" is an abbreviation for the French words that mean "Respond, if you please."

It's usually best to send the invitations through the mail. I can also pass them out by hand if I am absolutely certain that someone won't see someone else get an invitation and feel left out.

Once the invitations have gone out, it's time to plan.

A party is usually more fun with games, and games usually help guests get to know each other better. Sometimes I like to have silly games where everyone gets active. Other times we play guessing games or just talk. One time we even acted out a story! The most important thing about a party game is that everyone should be able to take part.

Food for a party can be almost anything. Ice cream and cake is usual for a birthday party, but I had a friend who had a birthday watermelon, complete with candles! I can serve my guests pretzels and soda, or we can have a complete meal. But I need to think ahead to make sure I'll have enough for everybody and also that everyone will have a place to sit while they eat. (Aunt Evelyn always says that half of what makes a party fun is careful planning.)

Mom and Dad and I always work together to make the food and put up the decorations. (I help them when they have parties, too.) And of course I pitch in to get the house looking nice and clean. It's not fair (and not polite) to have all the fun and leave Mom and Dad with all the work!

It's Partytime!

When the time for my party finally rolls around, sometimes I feel nervous. Aunt Evelyn says it's all right to feel this way. That just means I care about my guests and my party and I want everyone to have fun.

She must be right. We always seem to have fun!

I want to make sure everybody at my party feels special. I greet all my guests at the door and make sure they know everybody else. If they have brought a gift (either because it's a birthday party or just to be nice) I say a big thank you, and I set it aside until later. Then I show them around and try to make sure they feel welcome.

Once everyone is there, I try to make sure no one feels left out. If I spot someone standing alone in a corner, I go over and talk to her. I explain the games and let everyone know what there is to eat or drink. And even though it is my party and I planned it, I try not to act bossy and tell everyone what to do. If my party is a birthday party, there will probably be a time when I open the presents my friends have brought me. There's a nice way to do this. I should open each present, say out loud who it's from, read any card, then open the present and hold it up so that everyone can see. Then I say another great big thank you (and I'll write a thank-you note later).

When it's time for the party to end, I always go to the door with each guest as she leaves. I thank my guests for coming and thank them again for any gift they brought.

I also like to give the guests at my parties little favors or gifts to help them remember my party. These don't have to be fancy or expensive, but they should be a way to tell them, "Thanks for coming. I'm really glad you did."

When I'm Invited

If I'm the one invited to a party, the first thing I need to do is respond promptly to the invitation—to say yes or no. (It's nice to do this even if the invitation doesn't say RSVP.) If the party-giver invites me by phone, I can just answer right then or call her back to give an answer.

If the invitation was written, I need to call the number on the card. It's not enough just to see the party-giver in the hall at school and say, "I want to come."

If the invitation is for a birthday party, of course, I'll usually want to bring a present. For a casual party with friends, it's all right just to bring myself...and a fun attitude.

What should I wear to a party? Sometimes the invitation will say "casual," "dressy," or even "costume." Or sometimes the kind of party it is will tell me what to do. (I would never wear a frilly dress to go horseback riding.) If I'm not sure, the best thing to do is call the friend who is giving the party and ask!

How to Be a Good Partygoer

When the day of the party arrives, my most important job is to have a good time. But I can also do a lot to help others have a good time, too, and help the party go smoothly. And of course, I want to make my host and hostesses feel glad they invited me.

If it's a birthday party, I should start off the party by saying "Happy birthday" to the guest of honor as I hand over my gift.

After that, I should introduce myself to people I don't know and talk to people who look lonely. It's important to participate happily in the games and the activities and to be a good sport if I lose. I don't complain about the food, the favors, or anything else.

Although parties are famous for having fun food, that doesn't mean I should forget my mealtime manners. In fact, I think nice manners make a party special, so I always try to pay attention to sitting up straight, chewing with my mouth closed, and eating neatly. I try not to load up my plate, especially if others haven't been served yet.

Sometimes I feel nervous at a party, especially if I don't know everyone. Aunt Evelyn says I can help that nervous feeling by looking for someone else who looks a little lost and talking to her. I can also offer to help my hostess pass out food or drinks—having something to do helps with those nervous butterflies.

What if I do something embarrassing at a party? What if I spill something or trip somebody or break something? I need to remember that accidents can happen to anybody. I should simply apologize and maybe help my host or hostess clean up the mess. If I've broken something or stained something, it's polite to ask if I can help pay for it. But once the problem is taken care of, I should forget about it. I don't want to ruin the party talking on and on about a problem!

Finally, when it's time to go, I make sure I find my host and her parents and say that I had a good time. Then when I get home, it's nice to write a note or card that says another thank you.

A Theme for Your Party

Parties are extra fun if you plan them around a theme. You can make food and decorations to go with it—and you can even ask your guests to participate by coming in costume or bringing something to contribute to the theme. Here are some other ideas for fun party themes:

A Piggy Party
(everyone wear pink!)

A Skating Costume Party

A Mexican Christmas (with a piñata)

An Angelic Caroling Party (with angel costumes)

On the Farm

A Pink Valentine Party

A Monopoly Marathon (or a Scrabble Soiree)

A Pet Party

An Olympics Party

A Japanese Tea

A Pizza-Making Party (or a Bread-Baking Party)

A Cowgirl Cookout

Grownup Parties & Family Parties

Not every party I go to involves just children. Sometimes I help at grownup parties my parents give. Sometimes we go together to parties where there are both adults and children. Once I was the flower girl at a wedding, and I got to go to the rehearsal dinner and the reception. (That was really fun—I even caught the bouquet!)

If the party is at my house, I like to help greet the guests and take their coats. I also help serve the food and clean up, and I try to entertain any children that have come to the party, even little kids. If the party goes past my bedtime, I usually just say a polite goodnight to everyone and go to my room (or sometimes my parents let me stay up until everyone leaves).

If I am a guest at a grownup party, I try not to be loud or rowdy. I speak politely when I am spoken to and try to take an interest in what is going on. Sometimes it is all right for me to go outside and play with other children or watch TV in another room, but I should always ask first.

Sometimes at grownup parties I can't find a place to put my refreshments. It's hard to just sit in a chair and try to eat from a plate and drink from a cup! But Aunt Evelyn gave me some tips about this.

One thing I can do is leave room on my plate for my cup. Then I can put the plate on my lap and keep everything together. Another thing I can do is use another chair. This is a good possibility when the party is in a place where there are many folding chairs. Sometimes, if I look hard, I can even find a little table somewhere, or I can sit on the floor if it's carpeted. It's always a good idea to ask an adult before doing this, though.

The end of a grownup party is really just like the end of any party. It's a time for friendly goodbyes and happy thank you's. Everyone is tired but smiling, because it's been a wonderful celebration.

I just can't wait until it's party time again!

BEING A GUEST AT A PARTY PLACE

If I am attending a party at an amusement park, a pizza restaurant, or some other place outside my hosts home, a few special manners-rules apply. For one thing, it's important to stay with the group and not to wander off. It's not very courteous to make my hosts have to hunt for me. If we are given tokens to play games, I should keep track of my tokens and not ask for more. If an employee of the park helps with the party, I should remember to say thank you to her as well as to my hosts.

6 | "Thank You Very, Very Much"
GRATEFUL GOOD MANNERS

"Thank you" is one of those magic manners words—it makes everybody feel a little bit happier.

When I thank someone for doing something nice for me—sending me a nice present or cooking dinner for me or doing me a special favor—that person feels appreciated. He feels glad that he did something nice, and he may want to keep on doing nice things.

But that's just part of the thank-you magic.

You see, saying thank you also makes me feel better. It helps me remember the nice thing the other person did for me and to feel lucky that someone cared. I also feel good just because I remembered to say "thank you!"

"Thank you" is such powerful magic that Aunt Evelyn says it's impossible to have too much in our lives. She says learning to develop a thankful heart and to express our appreciation is the very heart of grateful good manners.

In Person and in Writing

When is a good time to say thank you?

Whenever anyone gives me a compliment, the right thing for me to say is "thanks."

When someone helps me with a project or does me a favor, that's the right time to say "thank you," too.

Any time I visit or eat dinner or spend the night at a friend's house, I should remember to thank her and her parents for their hospitality. I should thank my host and hostess at a party.

And of course, I should thank anyone who gives me a gift.

How do I say thank you?

Sometimes it's enough to just say the words in person. That's true when my friend says she likes my dress or my brother helps me carry a package to the car.

But if someone has sent me a gift or done something especially nice, an in-person thank you just isn't enough. I also need to send that person a written thank-you note.

Some people think thank-you notes are old-fashioned. They say it's easier just to say thank you in person or call the giver on the phone. And I guess it's better to say thank you that way than not to say it at all.

But there's something special about a letter that says "thank you." People can keep a letter. They can read and reread your words in your own handwriting.

Somehow a written note helps make the thank-you more real. It's almost like giving a gift back to the person who did something nice for you.

I don't think thank-you notes are old-fashioned at all!

It is important to write a thank-you note as soon as possible after I receive the gift or get home from the party. If I wait too long, I may forget to write at all! So I like to sit down and write thank you notes the very next day.

Aunt Evelyn says this is the very best thing to do. In fact, she thinks that learning to say thank-you in writing is so important that she gave me my own box of stationery with my name on it. It's beautiful—a box of pretty white paper with my initials and a yellow gingham border. When she gave that to me, I couldn't wait to use it...to write her a thank-you note!

FIVE GOOD REASONS TO WRITE A THANK-YOU NOTE

1. It's the right thing to do.

2. It helps me remember the gift and feel more grateful.

3. It's like giving a gift back.

4. If the gift came in the mail, it lets the giver know you received it.

5. (a selfish one) People who receive thank-you notes want to give more gifts!

How to Say It

Thank you notes don't have to be long or complicated. They don't even have to be spelled perfectly. But they should sound really thankful. And they should be a little more interesting than:

> Dear Grandma:
>
> Thank you for the present.
>
> Love, Emilie Marie

Aunt Evelyn says it's easy to write good thank-you notes if I remember to do three things.

First, I should mention the gift by name. In other words, instead of saying "the present" I should say "the jewelry-making kit" or the "crocheted vest." If I want to, I say what I liked best about the gift.

Second, I should talk about the time and effort and work the giver put into the gift. If Aunt Phyllis sent me a knitted sweater, I should talk about how hard she worked to make it. If my friend Jessica made me a clay animal, I should talk about that. If another friend went out and bought me a Barbie doll, I should talk about her taking the trouble to go out and get me a gift.

Third, I should talk about how I used the gift or how I want to use it. (If I'm not sure, I could say how I might use it.)

Here are some examples of good thank-you notes:

> Dear Aunt Evelyn:
> I just love the beautiful stationery you sent me. Thank you so much. I can't wait to use it.
> In fact, I'm using it to write this thank-you note! I also want to thank you for letting me visit you again. I always have fun at your house, and I learn a lot, too. I can't wait to visit again. I love you very much.
>
> Love, Emilie Marie

> Dear Mrs. Otto:
> I want to thank you for letting me spend the night with Donna. Your house is pretty and comfortable, and you were nice to have me.
>
> Sincerely, Emilie Marie

> Dear Jessica:
> Thanks for the birthday gift. I really love the little teddy bear with pajamas. He's already sitting on my bed. You were nice to give him to me. I hope you had fun at my party.
>
> Your friend, Emilie Marie